JOHN
JAMES
AUDUBON

John J Audubon

JOHN JAMES AUDUBON

Wildlife Artist

by
Peter Anderson

A First Book
Franklin Watts
A Division of Grolier Publishing
New York / London / Hong Kong / Sydney
Danbury, Connecticut

Cover photograph copyright ©: The Bettmann Archive.

Photographs copyright ©: The Bettmann Archive: pp. 2, 13, 22, 55;
Kentucky Department of Parks, John James Audubon Museum: pp. 10, 12, 28, 33, 37, 43, 49,
56, 59; North Wind Picture Archives: pp. 15, 19; The New York Historical Society: pp. 17, 50;
National Museum of American Art, Smithsonian Institution: p. 24;
Filson Club Historical Society: p. 30; Art Resource: pp. 52 (Scala/Art Resource, NY), 46
(Victoria & Albert Museum, London/Art Resource, NY).

Library of Congress Cataloging-in-Publication Data

Anderson, Peter, 1956–
John James Audubon : wildlife artist / by Peter Anderson.
p. cm. — (A First book)
Includes bibliographical references (p.) and index.
Summary: A biography of the nineteenth-century ornithologist, naturalist, and artist
famous for his accurate paintings of birds and animals.
ISBN 0-531-20202-X (lib. bdg.) — ISBN 0-531-15762-8 (pbk.)
1. Audubon, John James, 1785–1851 — Juvenile literature.
2. Ornithologists — United States — Biography — Juvenile literature.
3. Animal painters — United States — Biography — Juvenile literature.
[1. Audubon, John James, 1785–1851. 2. Naturalists. 3. Artists.]
I. Title. II. Series.
QL31.A9A68 1995
598'.092 — dc20
[B]
95-2597
CIP AC

6 5   62

CONTENTS

JOHN
JAMES
AUDUBON

Audubon's magnificent painting of the American flamingo

ACROSS THE OCEAN

Ever since I was a boy, I have had an astonishing desire to see the world and acquire a knowledge of birds.
—John James Audubon

For as long as he could remember, John James Audubon had heard his father's stories of pirates, of battles fought with the British and Spanish, of tropical islands in the West Indies. Now, at the age of eighteen, young Audubon was ready for his own adventure at sea. As the captain barked out commands, sailors tugged on ropes, and sea gulls swirled above the ship's rising sails, young

Jean Audubon, John James Audubon's father

Audubon waved to his family, who had come to bid him farewell.

Jean Audubon, the young man's father, was silent and thoughtful as he watched his boy's ship leave the harbor. He was reminded of the ocean crossings he had made as a French navy officer and later as a merchant and trader. Now it was his son's turn to cross the Atlantic.

Once in America, John James was to live on the farm his father owned in Pennsylvania. There, Jean Audubon knew his son would be safe from the war that France and England were soon to fight. Maybe he would learn how to farm. Perhaps he could learn how to speak English, something he had never been able to do in school. John James had never cared for school. He preferred "to go with...friends in search of birds' nests, or to fish and shoot."

Young Audubon was especially fond of birds. Often he would return home after school with his lunch basket full of feathers, eggs, and nests. Glad to see that his son had developed an interest, Jean Audubon gave John James a book of bird illustrations that inspired the boy to draw his own pictures. Even though his son's early drawings were rough and clumsy, Jean still encouraged him, and John James continued to draw.

Now, as his ship sailed down the Loire River and out into the open sea, John James thought little of his family. He stood beneath the billowing white

As a young man, John James Audubon
left his home in France and sailed to America.

sails, breathing in the salty air. In this new world of sky and sea, Audubon was overcome, he later wrote, with "an intense and indescribable pleasure."

That would soon change. As the ship sailed out into the Atlantic Ocean, huge white-capped rollers crashed into the bow and splashed over onto the deck. The big ship rocked up and down, twisting and turning as the waves surged underneath it. John James began to feel dizzy and his stomach ached. For days, he hung his head over the ship's rail, as sick as he had ever been.

Eventually, Audubon grew accustomed to the ship's rolling motion. Once again, he was able to appreciate all the activity and excitement around him. As a young boy growing up in France, he had seen ships like this only from a distance. Now he could hear the captain's words. He could feel the wind shift. He could watch the sailors as they climbed in the rope-ladder rigging above the deck, racing back and forth to adjust the sails.

Near the top of the mast was a platform called a crow's nest where the lookout scanned the waters ahead for other ships and distant lands. As the weeks passed, the scene before them changed little. Audubon was beginning to feel like the ocean would roll on forever. Then one day he heard the lookout's cry. Soon he saw the dark line of America's coast on the horizon.

INTO THE FOREST

CHAPTER TWO

Hunting, fishing, and draw-
ing . . . occupied my every
moment. Cares I knew not.
—John James Audubon

In 1803, John James finally arrived at Mill Grove, Jean Audubon's farm in Pennsylvania. From the farmhouse on top of the hill he could look out over much of his father's land. Perkiomen Creek flowed out of a deep, forested ravine and trailed out across the wide meadow below him.

Audubon loved tramping through the wild lands around Perkiomen Creek. "Hunting, fishing, and drawing . . . occupied my every moment," he

John James Audubon

later wrote of his early days at Mill Grove. "Cares I knew not."

Each morning he rose early. As he walked out across the meadows, the grass was still wet with dew. Kingfishers flew through the mist rising up from the creek. Red-winged blackbirds flickered through the marshlands. Bald eagles soared overhead.

Climbing through the boulders above the creek one day, Audubon noticed a small nest built on a rocky ledge. Underneath the nest, an opening in the rock wall turned out to be the entrance to a cave that became his favorite hideaway. Wandering in the woods, he often paused there to write or draw.

One spring morning he heard wings rustling above him. He looked up and saw a pair of phoebes who had returned to their nest near the cave entrance. He watched them as they flew in and out of the cave hunting insects. It wasn't long before there were several eggs in the nest—"eggs so white and transparent," Audubon wrote, "that the sight was more pleasant . . . than if they had been diamonds of the same size."

By the time the young birds hatched, the older phoebes had grown accustomed to Audubon. "They would come in close by me," he said, "as if I were only a post." Being able to watch the birds so closely inspired him to try to capture their graceful move-

Audubon's illustration of a phoebe. As his artistic skills grew, Audubon was able to sketch and paint more-realistic portraits of the birds he loved to watch.

ments in his drawings. He outlined hundreds of sketches over the next few weeks, but was unable to finish them. Being close to the birds wasn't enough. Their constant motion made them difficult models. For now, Audubon's hope of re-creating them on paper was beyond his ability.

It was even harder to examine other birds as they flashed through the forest. How was he to draw these birds if he couldn't study them? He had to have a model or a specimen. The solution, for him, was hunting. As wild birds seemed to be abundant, he saw no harm in killing specimens. How else could he accurately re-create the patterns in a feather, or the curve of a beak, or the color of an eye?

Yet even with specimens, the task of making an accurate picture proved difficult. He wanted to celebrate the life of the bird in his art, but he couldn't seem to do that with the birds that he had killed and preserved. He could capture the details of the birds' appearance, but he couldn't draw them in a pose that looked natural. He tried fastening threads to his models so that he could raise or lower a head, or a tail, or hold a wing in place. Still he wasn't satisfied.

For almost a month, he was so discouraged that he gave up drawing. Then he had an idea. Rising early one morning, he galloped his horse into the nearby village of Norristown. There he bought a

The Audubon home in Mill Grove, Pennsylvania

supply of wire, which he took back to his studio at Mill Grove. Running pieces of the wire through the wings and legs of the birds that he had preserved, he was able to arrange them in more realistic poses.

By the time one of his neighbors came by for a visit later that year, Audubon's room looked like a museum. In addition to the stuffed birds, "the walls were festooned with all sorts of bird's eggs, carefully blown out and strung on a thread," the neighbor said. "The chimney piece was covered with stuffed squirrels, raccoons and opossums; and the shelves around were likewise crowded with specimens, among which were fishes, frogs, snakes, lizards and other reptiles. Besides these stuffed varieties, many paintings were arrayed on the wall, chiefly of birds."

Audubon was learning but he wouldn't be satisfied until his illustrations thrilled him as much as a bird flying through the forest.

LOVE AND MONEY

Lucy . . . seemed radiant with beauty. . . . I was pleased to believe that [she] looked upon me as a not very strange animal.
—John James Audubon

During his first year at Mill Grove, Audubon spent much of his time alone. He rarely visited neighbors until he met William Bakewell hunting along the banks of Perkiomen Creek one winter day. As they followed their hunting dogs through the tall pines, Bakewell and Audubon had a chance to get acquainted. John James accepted an invitation to visit the Bakewell farm.

Lucy Bakewell Audubon

The day that he went to call on William Bakewell and his family was a day that Audubon would never forget. When John James arrived at his neighbor's farmhouse, he met Bakewell's oldest daughter, Lucy. As they sat beside a cheerful fire waiting for her father, Lucy charmed young Audubon with her gentle nature and graceful good looks.

Like her father, Lucy Bakewell was intelligent and well mannered. She spoke with an appealing English accent, choosing her words carefully. As they talked quietly beside the fire, Audubon secretly hoped that her father would be slow in coming.

Lucy knew of Audubon only because of his reputation. She had heard of the young Frenchman's zest for hunting and love of birds. Now she could feel the passion in the words he used to describe his life at Mill Grove, even though speaking English was still a struggle for him. His wild, long-haired appearance only added to his mystique.

In the months that followed, Audubon took every opportunity to visit the Bakewells, hoping to charm Lucy as she had charmed him. He invited the Bakewells to Mill Grove where they were treated to a feast of pheasant and partridge followed by an afternoon of skating on Perkiomen Creek. Much to Lucy's delight, Audubon whisked her across the ice on a sled. There wasn't much he wouldn't have done to impress her. On

An example of Audubon's early artwork. Despite his talent, John James Audubon would struggle for many years before being able to make a living as an artist.

another skating date, he dashed back and forth on the ice carrying his rifle. When Lucy's brother Thomas threw his hat in the air, John James shot it full of holes.

By spring, John James and Lucy were in love. William Bakewell began to hear troubling rumors. Someone had seen Lucy climbing into a cave above Perkiomen Creek with the young Frenchman. Bakewell was relieved to find out that they had only been watching Audubon's favorite phoebes. Still, there was reason for concern.

It was clear that Lucy was drawn to Audubon as he was to her. What if they were to marry? William Bakewell knew that John James cared little about anything besides nature and his artwork. He certainly didn't care much for farming. How, Bakewell wondered, would Audubon ever be able to support Lucy?

Audubon hoped that his efforts to revive an old lead mine at Mill Grove would bring him the money needed to marry and support Lucy Bakewell. Despite his best intentions, it never paid off. Then, in the winter of 1805, Audubon was unable to work because of an illness that kept him bedridden. With the help of Lucy's tender care, he gradually recovered. That same winter, he received word from France that his father had also been ill.

In March 1805, as soon as Audubon was strong enough to travel, he left the Bakewells to visit his ailing father. After his second ocean crossing, Audubon arrived at his boyhood home in Coueron, France, delighted to find his father healthy once again. He told Jean Audubon excitedly of his new life — of sailing the ocean, of the many places he had explored around the farm, of all the birds and animals, of the Bakewells, and of Lucy.

As Jean Audubon listened patiently to his son's stories, he realized that John James had not yet learned to support himself, let alone a wife. Young Audubon's pursuits had more to do with birds than business. For Jean Audubon, who was having money struggles of his own, continued support of John James would be difficult. Under these circumstances, he could hardly agree to his son's marriage.

If John James was to marry Lucy Bakewell, he would have to learn to make a living. Although his son had never demonstrated any ability in business, perhaps with the right partner he could learn. At least, that was Jean Audubon's hope.

Arrangements were made for John James to return to Mill Grove with Ferdinand Rozier, a business-minded young man who had served in the French navy. It was agreed that they would sell off the Audubon farm and use the proceeds to set up their own business. What that business would be was left for the two young Frenchmen to decide.

CHAPTER FOUR

ON TO THE FRONTIER

Louisville extends along the river for seven or eight miles. . . . The rumbling sound of the waters, as they tumble over the rock paved bed of the rapids, is at all times soothing to the ear. Fish and game are abundant. But above all, the generous hospitality of the inhabitants . . . had induced me to fix upon it as a place of residence.
— John James Audubon

On April 5, 1808, three weeks before his twenty-third birthday, John James Audubon married Lucy Bakewell in the parlor of the farmhouse where they had first met. Three days later they were bound for the frontier town of Louisville, Kentucky. There young

Ferdinand Rozier was Audubon's
business partner in Louisville, Kentucky.

Audubon and his partner, Ferdinand Rozier, had already set up a dry goods store.

William Bakewell knew that Audubon was still inexperienced despite a business apprenticeship in New York City. The success of his store was uncertain, but Bakewell was sure of Lucy's devotion to the marriage. And even if he lacked confidence in Audubon, he still found him to be a likable young man.

For Audubon and his young bride, the journey west was anything but a honeymoon. For fifteen hours each day, their stagecoach rumbled over rocky roads. On the third day, the road into the Allegheny Mountains became so steep that many of the passengers, including Audubon, had to get out and walk.

Audubon was just far enough away to avoid injury when Lucy's coach lurched over a huge boulder and crashed onto its side. He looked on helplessly as the frightened horses bolted ahead, dragging the overturned stagecoach. When the driver finally caught them, Audubon rushed to the aid of his wife, who was badly bruised and shaken.

Fortunately for Lucy, who had never been fond of traveling, their journey down the Ohio River wasn't nearly as rough. In Pittsburgh, they crowded onto a flatboat along with hundreds of other passengers. Cattle, horses, wagons—anything useful for a new life on the frontier—cluttered the deck. As

Audubon and his young bride arrived in Louisville, a bustling and rapidly growing city on the western frontier of the United States.

their boat drifted down the river, Lucy often took refuge in one of the two small cabins where women and children huddled together for warmth. Audubon seemed oblivious to the weather. Even in the wind and rain he scanned the riverbanks and searched the skies for birds.

When they finally docked in Louisville, Lucy's gaze wandered up to the rows of red brick homes and stores that were perched on the bluff above them. Downstream, the river boiled and churned for several miles as it cascaded over ledges of limestone. Many boats stopped here to hire seasoned river pilots who could guide them through the falls below town. That meant more trade for merchants like Audubon and Rozier.

As John James led his bride up the hill to their new home, all the introductions convinced Lucy that there wasn't one person in Louisville that her husband hadn't met. Although they hadn't been in business long, John James and his partner, Ferdinand, seemed to work well together. At first, Rozier was content to mind the store and keep the books. Audubon was more interested in meeting the townsfolk and drumming up business.

Still, Audubon's love of birds often took precedence over everything else. One day, he let his horse stray off with a saddlebag full of money while he followed an unusual species of warbler into the brush. There were those around town, Ferdinand Rozier among them, who began to think that Audubon cared more about birds than business.

Meanwhile, Lucy was the big news over at the Indian Queen Hotel where she and Audubon lived. She had never imagined herself living in a hotel full of frontiersmen. But in a town where housing was scarce, she realized it would have to do. At least John James had arranged for a private apartment. Still, the Audubons often had their meals with the other hotel residents, some of whom noticed that Lucy was soon to be a mother.

There were plenty of congratulations offered when the Audubons announced the birth of their first son, Victor. John James was thrilled. For a month or so, he showered his wife and newborn son with most of his attention.

Meanwhile, Ferdinand Rozier took over most of the responsibilities for their dry goods store. Profits, if any, were small. Rozier began to wonder if they would fare better in a smaller town with fewer competitors. Audubon suggested they relocate to Henderson, Kentucky, a frontier river town 125 miles (200 km) downstream.

For Lucy, the only consolation of the move to Henderson was a small log cabin—finally a home of

John James Audubon painted this 1822
portrait of his son Victor.

their own. The town itself was much smaller than Louisville. It was so small that there seemed to be hardly enough people to support a store. While Rozier waited patiently for the occasional customer, Audubon made sure there was food on their table. "Guns and fishing lines," Audubon later said, "were our principal means of support." It wasn't long before there was talk of another move, this time with winter approaching.

CHAPTER FIVE

STORMY TIMES

The waters were unusually low, the thermometer indicated excessive cold, the earth all around was covered with snow, dark clouds were spread over the heavens, and . . . all appearances were unfavorable to a speedy prosecution of our voyage.

—John James Audubon

In December 1809, after making arrangements for Lucy and Victor to stay with a neighbor, Audubon, Rozier, and several crewmen boarded a keelboat and set out on the Ohio River again. Working the current with a 60-foot (18-m) sweep oar, they figured on reaching the Mississippi River town of

St. Genevieve in several days. At least that was their plan.

As snow fell from a dark December sky, they rounded the first big bend in the Ohio River, and the village of Henderson slipped away behind them. Huge chunks of ice floated past snow-covered riverbanks. The current seemed slow and getting slower.

On Christmas Eve, wind and snow forced them to make camp 6 miles (10 km) above the joining of the Ohio and the Mississippi rivers. At a riverside feast on Christmas Day, they shared a meal of bear fat and nut soup with a band of Shawnee Indians.

By daybreak on December 26 they were back on the river. Progress was slow—ice floes had all but choked off the river downstream. As they neared the point where the Ohio and the Mississippi rivers met, the ice thickened. The wind blew hard, and again it began to snow. They decided to set aside their oars and build a shelter beside the river. There, they would wait for a thaw.

As they unloaded barrels of whiskey, gunpowder, and other supplies bound for the new store in St. Genevieve, Ferdinand Rozier worried that they would be stranded until spring. Audubon showed little concern. The woods, after all, were full of wild game—deer, turkeys, raccoons, and opossums were

After breaking with business partner Ferdinand Rozier,
Audubon returned to run his store in Henderson,
Kentucky. His family lived in this house.

seen near camp, and a flock of swans had settled in on the icy river nearby.

As the days passed and the ice grew thicker, Audubon amused himself and a visiting band of Osage Indians with his artwork. His drawings of familiar birds and animals impressed them, as did his portraits. "When I made a . . . likeness of one of the Indians," he later said, "they cried out with astonishment and laughed."

But Ferdinand Rozier found little to be cheered by. Supplies intended for their store were dwindling, and there was no sign of a thaw. Audubon's lack of concern only added to his anxiety. Then late one February night, the partners' predicament suddenly changed.

"Get up! Get up! The ice is breaking," cried the keelboat pilot. "Hurry or we may lose her." Fountains of water surged upward as the frozen river cracked open. Great hunks of ice rose and sank like whales. Everyone ran down to the keelboat, carrying whatever they could find to shield it from the icy tumult.

At daybreak, they heard a thundering roar downstream. The ice dam that had trapped them for six weeks had finally broken through. Within hours they were steering the keelboat back into the current. But underneath the excitement and relief of escape, there was tension between Audubon and

Rozier. The ordeal of the winter seemed to have strained their partnership.

Shortly after their arrival in St. Genevieve, Audubon and Rozier decided to part company. Considering their differences, it was remarkable that they had stayed partners as long as they had. To Audubon, Rozier seemed narrow-minded. "I rarely passed a day without drawing a bird or noting its habits," John James later said. "Rozier cared only for money."

Audubon, said Rozier, "had no taste for commerce and was continually in the forest."

Partly because of unpaid loans and an inability to consistently support Lucy, many of the Bakewells agreed with Rozier. Audubon "neglects his material interests, and is forever wasting his time hunting, drawing, and stuffing birds," one of them said. "We fear that he will never be fit for any practical purpose."

Despite his reputation, Audubon finally showed that he was capable of running a business. For almost eight years after returning to Henderson in the spring of 1811, his store earned him a comfortable living. Then, in 1819, he had a streak of bad luck. He made some bad investments. A weak economy added to his difficulties, and his debts mounted. Finally, he was arrested and jailed for his debts and forced to declare bankruptcy.

All of this was a hard blow to Audubon, but he wasn't one to waste time. After he was released from jail, Audubon managed to eke out a living lettering signs and painting portraits in Louisville. All the while he was drawing new birds.

When he took the job of curator at the Western Museum of Natural History in Cincinnati, he hoped that he would finally be able to make his living as a naturalist and an artist. Unfortunately, the museum ran out of money and was unable to pay him. Once again, Audubon wondered what to do next.

CHAPTER SIX

DRIFTING TOWARD THE DREAM

On the opposite shore of the Mississippi vast alluvial beds stretched along towards the dense forest beyond. The way the sunbeams fell on distant objects was peculiarly pleasing. As I watched the motion of the whiteheaded eagle in pursuit of the fish hawk, my mind filled with the wonderful ways of that Power to whom I too owe my existence.

—John James Audubon

On an October afternoon in 1820, Audubon hugged his wife and children one last time before leaving Cincinnati on a flatboat bound for New Orleans. He traveled light, taking only his gun, his art supplies, a

Throughout his life, John James Audubon
felt more at home in the natural world
than he did in the business world.

book or two, a telescope, and the clothes on his back. His pockets were empty. "Without any money," he wrote in his journal, "my talents are to be my support."

Over the years, admirers of Audubon's bird drawings had suggested he try to publish them. With encouragement from Lucy and friends at the museum in Cincinnati, Audubon had decided to pursue that dream. Publishing and selling a complete collection of North American bird drawings, he hoped, would lift him out of poverty once and for all.

During his journey to New Orleans, Audubon planned to add new species to his collection of drawings. With him was Joseph Mason, a talented thirteen-year-old artist and botanist who would draw the backgrounds for Audubon's new bird portraits.

At dusk, watching the bats chase insects above the Ohio River diverted Audubon's attention for a while. But as the shadows grew deeper and darker along the banks of the river, so did his thoughts. Would he really be able to support himself and his family in the coming months? How long until he would see them again?

Audubon's future seemed as murky as the fog that cloaked the Mississippi River as they drifted farther south. Nevertheless, he marveled at the variety of bird life he and Mason saw as they rowed a little skiff out ahead of the big flatboat each day. Owls hooted along the riverbanks at night. Ducks and geese were following the river south for winter. Flocks of pelicans whirled over islands and sandbars.

By the time they pulled into the river town of Natchez, Mississippi, Audubon had added fifteen new species to his collection of more than two hundred bird illustrations. Each new portrait helped him fight off periods of self-doubt, eased the pain of separation from his family, and assured him that he was drifting closer to his dream. But the doubts and darkness returned with a vengeance when he realized, after leaving Natchez, that his portfolio of new drawings was missing. They must have been left behind on the docks.

Audubon's bad luck continued when he was robbed shortly after his arrival in New Orleans. To make matters worse, work was scarce. Only after days of wandering the city streets was he able to find a job with a local portrait painter.

Meanwhile Lucy was losing patience. Since marrying Audubon, she had suffered through plenty of hardship, rarely voicing a complaint. She had been sympathetic to Audubon's ambition and had put up with his wandering. But in March 1821, Lucy's father died. It was a difficult time to be on her own in a frontier town. The strain of raising and educating their two sons by herself was too much. No longer was she willing to put up with Audubon's inability to

Audubon's painting of his second son, John

support her. In a letter, she told him that she didn't want to see him until he had some meaningful accomplishments to show for all his time away.

Audubon was finally able to send Lucy some money, but making a living continued to be a struggle. He begged her to join him in New Orleans. Weeks passed without word from Lucy. He met every steamship that came down the river from Cincinnati but found only unfamiliar faces. Would he ever see his family again?

Finally, in December 1821, they arrived. After fourteen months of separation and doubt, the Audubon reunion next to the Mississippi River was a hopeful one. John James was still earning only a meager living painting family portraits and giving art lessons, activities that would continue to be his means of support while he was in Louisiana. Still, he was able to offer his family a home.

PILGRIM'S PROGRESS

I have labored like a carthorse for 30 years on a single work.
—John James Audubon

Despite their joyful reunion in New Orleans, Lucy Audubon knew that the time would come when she would be on her own again. She knew that Audubon would have to travel considerable distances to complete his collection of drawings. After Lucy found her first teaching job in Louisiana, she could at least rest assured that she would be able to support herself when he was gone.

Audubon's painting of belted kingfishers (the two top
birds are males; the bottom one is a female)

With Mason's help, Audubon had finished numerous bird portraits, but to find other species he would have to leave his family behind. In the years following Lucy's arrival in New Orleans and Mason's return to Cincinnati, Audubon worked his way up and down the Mississippi River. Often, he was able to find temporary work as an art instructor.

As he traveled, his collection of drawings grew as did his skill as an artist. In 1824, Audubon traveled all the way to Philadelphia and New York, hoping to publish his collection. In Philadelphia, some of his writings on birds were accepted for publication by a natural history journal. In New Jersey, he had one of his drawings published for the first time. But his dream remained unrealized.

By the time Audubon came home to Louisiana, he had come up with a new strategy for publishing his bird illustrations. It was a plan that Lucy supported despite the fact that it would mean another long separation. Still, she believed enough in Audubon and his work to contribute part of her teaching salary to his cause. After a year of saving up his own wages from tutoring, Audubon gathered up his drawings. If he couldn't publish them in America, he would take them elsewhere. With Lucy's blessing, he set sail for England.

WOODSMAN IN ENGLAND

CHAPTER EIGHT

Mr. Audubon, the people here don't know who you are at all. But depend on it, they shall know
— W. H. Lizars

Audubon felt timid and lonely as he walked through the streets of Liverpool in July 1826. In the fog and rain, the city seemed gloomy. Already, he missed the Louisiana countryside. But the hospitality of the people he met soon made up for his first impressions of England.

With several letters of introduction from friends back in America, Audubon introduced himself

This Audubon painting of purple grackles was
printed by W. H. Lizars, one of England's
foremost printmakers at the time.

In their later years, the Audubons
lived in this house near New York City.

around Liverpool. With his walking stick, his long hair, and his fringed buckskin clothes, Audubon looked the part of the wild frontiersman.

In the drawing rooms of Liverpool, he played up his frontier image—imitating bird calls, singing Ohio River songs, answering endless questions and making sketches of the American landscape, its animals, and the Indians. The frontier artist's reputation spread rapidly, soon earning him celebrity status.

As his money supply dwindled, Audubon knew that popularity alone wouldn't be enough to get his work published. He would have to make the right contacts. In Edinburgh, he had the chance to meet W. H. Lizars, a well-known printmaker who reproduced art for illustrated books. When the printmaker agreed to look over Audubon's work, John James nervously unpacked one of his drawings. He knew that Lizars was an important man in the English book business.

Lizars leaped out of his chair, heaping praise on Audubon's work. He was especially fond of a drawing that pictured a mockingbird and a rattlesnake. Never had he seen anything like it. With great enthusiasm, Lizars agreed to engrave several bird portraits at a time. Meanwhile Audubon would sell subscriptions to the series to pay off the printing costs. He knew his role as the salesman would be a

The Blue Heron or Crane

difficult one. The prints were expensive, limiting his customers to the wealthy. But what did he have to lose? "If I do not succeed," he wrote in his journal, "I can return to my woods and there in peace and quiet, live and die."

So Audubon traveled all over England promoting his work. He even sold a subscription to King George IV. Still, no amount of success could help him shake the loneliness he felt. He missed his home and family. When he wrote Lucy of his progress and asked her to join him, she was reluctant. After all, he had been known to exaggerate before. Besides, if she were to join him, wasn't there a good possibility that he would leave her stranded once again?

By the time Audubon returned to America in May 1829, he was desperate to see his wife and family. But he was also desperate to pursue the completion of his dream. To raise money and complete new drawings to round out his collection, he felt as though he had to stay in New York and Philadelphia. Only after a great deal of pleading and persuasion did Lucy agree to join him. In April 1830, Lucy accompanied him back to England, where she provided the support that Audubon needed in the final phase of his lifelong quest.

JOURNEY'S END

To study nature was, to me, to ramble through her domains late and early. If I observed all as I should, I knew that the memory of what I saw would be of service to me.
—John James Audubon

Even though Audubon's projects were well under way by the time Lucy arrived in England, the years that lay ahead would be difficult ones. Despite several years of poor health, Lucy helped Audubon as he struggled to write descriptions to accompany his bird paintings. Meanwhile, Victor and John, their two sons, supervised printers and

A late photograph of John James Audubon,
who died at the age of sixty-six

helped with artwork. Finding enough subscribers to compensate for printing costs was a never-ending task.

In the fall of 1839, after almost thirteen years in England, Audubon came home with two published volumes: *The Birds of North America*, his collected drawings, and the *Ornithological Biography*, his notes and comments on each bird species. Finally, when he was fifty-four, Audubon's works began to earn him the recognition at home that he had been yearning for.

Still, it wasn't until he began to sell subscriptions for a smaller edition of his bird paintings that his financial condition improved enough to build Lucy a house on New York's Hudson River. After so many years as a rover, John James Audubon was glad to be home, but his love of travel had not left him altogether.

For years, he had wanted to go out west. Determined to realize that dream, Audubon joined a boatload of trappers in the spring of 1843, and traveled up the Missouri River to Yellowstone. The elk, the bighorn sheep, the buffalo, and the Indians who

In the late 1800s, a memorial to
John James Audubon was erected in New York.

followed the great herds—it was all so spectacular. To capture it all on paper was a daunting task.

"I began drawing at five this morning, and worked . . . till after three," he wrote in his journal one day. "Becoming fatigued for want of practice, I took a short walk, regretting I could no longer draw twelve or fifteen hours without a pause or thought of weariness."

Audubon's age was beginning to show. His desire hadn't changed. He shared the enthusiasm of the boy who began sketching birds in Coueron, France. He was as adventurous as the young man who explored the woods at Mill Grove. But he no longer had the stamina of the artist who had finished *The Birds of North America*.

By the time Audubon came home in the fall, he was exhausted. He had hoped to complete a volume of paintings on the mammals of North America. As his eyesight began to fail him, Audubon would leave that project for his sons to complete. And indeed they did, adding to the great legacy left behind by their father, who watched the birds fly south along the Hudson, one last time, in the fall of 1851.

FOR FURTHER
READING

Amdur, Richard. *Wilderness Preservation*. New York: Chelsea House Publishers, 1993.

Audubon, John James. *Capturing Nature: The Writings and Art of John James Audubon*. New York: Walker, 1993.

Brenner, Barbara. *On the Frontier with Mr. Audubon*. New York: Coward, McCann & Geoghegan, 1977.

Challand, Helen J. *Vanishing Forests*. Chicago: Childrens Press, 1991.

Faber, Doris. *Nature and the Environment*. New York: Scribner, 1991.

Hirsch, S. Carl. *Guardians of Tomorrow: Pioneers in Ecology*. New York: Viking Press, 1971.

Kastner, Joseph. *John James Audubon*. New York: Harry N. Abrams, 1992.

Keene, Ann T. *Earthkeepers: Observers and Protectors of Nature*. New York: Oxford University Press, 1994.

INDEX

Italicized page numbers
refer to illustrations.

ABOUT THE AUTHOR

Peter Anderson has worked as a river guide, carpenter, newspaper reporter, writing teacher, editor, and wilderness ranger. He has written ten books for young readers on topics related to nature, Native Americans, and the history of the American West. Currently, he lives in Salt Lake City, Utah.